Little Bible Heroes™
Moses

Written by Victoria Kovacs
Illustrated by David Ryley

NASHVILLE, TENNESSEE

GOLDQUILL
WWW.GOLDQUILL.CO.UK

fb.com/littlebibleheroes

Published 2017 by B&H Kids, a division of LifeWay Christian Resources, Nashville, Tennessee.
Text and illustrations copyright © 2017, GoldQuill, United Kingdom.
All rights reserved. Scripture quotations are taken from the Christian Standard Bible ®
Copyright © 2017 by Holman Bible Publishers. Used by permission.
ISBN: 978-1-4627-4339-1   Dewey Decimal Classification: CE
Subject Heading: MOSES \ JOHN, APOSTLE \ BIBLE STORIES
Printed November 2021 in Dongguan, Guangdong, China
3 4 5 6 7 8 • 25 24 23 22 21

Moses is tending sheep in the desert when he sees a burning bush. He hears God's voice calling to him from it.

"Moses! I am sending you to Pharaoh, and you will lead my people out of Egypt."

God's people are slaves in Egypt, where Pharaoh is the king.

Moses tells Pharaoh to let God's people go, but Pharaoh is hard-hearted and says no.

God sends ten awful plagues that hurt Egypt. One was a plague of frogs! Finally Pharaoh says God's people can leave Egypt.

When the people reach the edge of the Red Sea, they turn to see Pharaoh and his army chasing them in chariots and on horses. The people are trapped!

God tells Moses, "Lift your staff, reach out with your hand over the sea, and divide it in two."

Moses obeys, and God splits the water in half. The people cross to the other side on dry land!

Pharaoh's army begins to cross too, but God makes their chariot wheels swerve. He tells Moses to reach out his hand over the sea again. This time the water covers the Egyptians. Splash!

Moses and the people of Israel sing a song to God. They praise Him for rescuing them.

Read:

I will sing to the LORD, for he is highly exalted;
he has thrown the horse and its rider into the sea.
The LORD is my strength and my song.
—Exodus 15:1–2

Think:

1. How did God take care of Moses and His people?
2. What is your favorite song to sing to God?

Remember:

God takes care of the
people He loves!

Read:

And there are also many other things that Jesus did, which, if every one of them were written down, I suppose not even the world itself could contain the books that would be written.
—John 21:25

Think:

1. John wrote to tell people about Jesus. Do you like to write?
2. What are some ways you serve Jesus?

Remember:

You can tell people about Jesus too!

God gives John a special gift—
a glimpse into heaven. He
writes down what he sees so
we can read it too.

When he is older, John is banished to
an island for telling people about Jesus.
He writes about his time with Jesus.
The words he writes are in the Bible.

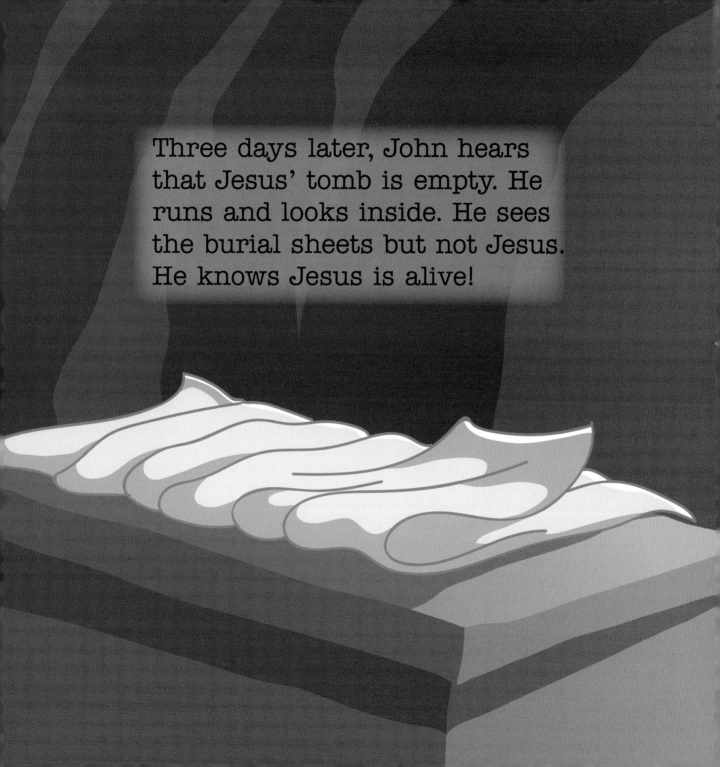

Three days later, John hears that Jesus' tomb is empty. He runs and looks inside. He sees the burial sheets but not Jesus. He knows Jesus is alive!

John is with Jesus' mother at the crucifixion. Jesus tells him, "This is your mother." From then on, John cares for her in his home.

At the Passover meal, Jesus says one of the disciples will betray Him. John leans against Jesus and asks, "Who is it?"

Jesus chooses John and eleven other men, called disciples, to travel with Him and preach. Jesus calls John His "beloved" because he is a good friend to Jesus.

John and his older brother, James, are fishermen. They are fixing nets in their boat when Jesus calls to them. They leave and follow Jesus.

Little Bible Heroes™
John

Written by Victoria Kovacs
Illustrated by David Ryley

B&H KIDS
NASHVILLE, TENNESSEE

GOLDQUILL
WWW.GOLDQUILL.CO.UK

fb.com/littlebibleheroes

Published 2017 by B&H Kids, a division of LifeWay Christian Resources, Nashville, Tennessee.
Text and illustrations copyright © 2017, GoldQuill, United Kingdom.
All rights reserved. Scripture quotations are taken from the Christian Standard Bible ®
Copyright © 2017 by Holman Bible Publishers. Used by permission.
ISBN: 978-1-4627-4339-1   Dewey Decimal Classification: CE
Subject Heading: MOSES \ JOHN, APOSTLE \ BIBLE STORIES
Printed November 2021 in Dongguan, Guangdong, China
3 4 5 6 7 8 • 25 24 23 22 21